CHEESE PLEASE!

EDITED BY JUDITH BOSLEY

DESIGNED AND ILLUSTRATED BY JILL ELLEN PARLING

Grand Books, Inc.
Middleton, Michigan 48856

Printed in the United States of America

Library of Congress Catalog Card Number: 86-80738

ISBN 0-930809-02-5

Grand Books Inc.
P.O. Box 7
Middleton, MI 48856

INDEX

Family Cheese Favorites

APPETIZERS

Family Cheese Favorites

1
Cheese Ball I

2 C sharp cheddar
8 oz. cream cheese
1 t lemon juice
2 tsp Worcestershire sauce
Dash tabasco sauce
1/2 C chopped nuts

Have ingredients at room temperature. Mix well. Shape into a ball, chill, roll in nuts to serve.

2
Cheese Ball II

8 oz. cream cheese
1 4 oz. glass blue cheese spread
1 4 oz. glass Old English spread
2 T dried parsley
Garlic salt, onion salt or other seasonings to taste
1/2 C chopped pecans

Mix ingredients, mixture will be soft. Sprinkle 1/2 of nuts on a foil sheet. Put cheese on nuts. Sprinkle rest of nuts on top and sides of ball. Wrap foil around and seal into a ball shape. Chill. Keeps very well. If only part of ball is used, more nuts may be added and ball reshaped.

3

Deep Fried Cheese I
Try this cocktail snack.

Cut COLD Camembert cheese in bite-sized wedges. Coat wedges with flour, dip in slightly beaten egg, and coat with fine bread crumbs. Refrigerate. Fry cheese 1½ minutes in very hot salad oil. Drain on paper towels. Serve hot.

4

Deep Fried Cheese II

Vegetable oil for deep frying
1 lb. cheese of choice
1 C biscuit mix
1/2 C milk
1 egg

Cut cheese in 3/4 inch cubes, insert round toothpick. Mix batter ingredients. Dip cheese in batter and fry, several at a time in oil 375 degrees. Drain and serve.

To prevent cheese from becoming stringy, either cook at high temperatures for a short time, or at low temperatures very slowly.

5

Saganaki
Opa!

1 lb. Kasseri or Kefalotiri cheese,
    cut into four serving size pieces,
    1/2 inch thick
Flour to coat cheese
2 T melted butter
2 T brandy
Juice of 1/2 lemon

Dust cheese slices with flour and place in a greased, small heavy skillet or pan with an oven proof handle. Pour melted butter over cheese and broil until cheese is very lightly browned and partially melted. Remove from broiler and pour brandy over cheese. Ignite brandy (very carefully, keeping hands and face away from flame.) When flame begins to burn out, squeeze lemon juice over pan and serve immediately. Serve with crusty bread. Serves 4.

6
Pan Fried Cheese

1½ lb. piece Gruyere cheese
Flour to coat cheese
1 egg
1 T water
1/2 C fine bread crumbs
2 T butter

Coat all cheese surfaces with flour. Beat egg with water. Dip cheese in egg, then in crumbs. Heat butter until foamy in small skillet. Cook cheese covered 5 minutes or until golden. Turn and fry other side. Make a cut in cheese so it will run on plate. Serve warm with french bread. Small sized cheese pieces can be fried with this method.

7

Cheese Toast
A go-with for spaghetti

1 C grated swiss cheese
1 egg yolk
1 T olive oil
1 T parsley or fresh dill
1/2 t paprika
Salt and pepper to taste
1 loaf French bread

Slice bread in 24 thin slices.
blend rest of ingredients and
spread on one side of each slice.
Bake cheese side up 5 minutes at
450 degrees. Watch closely!

8
Cheese Bites
Having a wine and cheese party?

Bread cut in 1" cubes
3 oz. cream cheese
1/4 lb. sharp cheddar
3/4 C butter
2 egg whites

Melt cheeses and butter in double
boiler. Let stand 10 minutes. Beat
egg whites and fold into cheese.
Dip bread cubes (crust removed)
into cheese until coated. Place on
cookie sheet and chill overnight.
(Can also freeze at this point.)
Bake at 400 degrees until puffy
and golden.

9
Garlic Cheese Roll

3 oz. cream cheese
4 slices pimento cheese
1 small clove garlic

Warm cheeses to room temperature. Mix and cream together.
Mash garlic, or put it through a
garlic press. Blend into cheeses.
Form cheese into 2 rolls about
four inches long. Roll each piece
in chili powder. Wrap in foil and
refrigerate to harden. Serve
sliced thinly on round crackers.

10
Clam Cream Dip

1 C creamed cottage cheese
3 oz. cream cheese
1 t Worcestershire sauce
8 oz. can clams, minced
3-4 T light cream
2 t prepared horseradish

Blend cheeses, horseradish and Worcestershire. Stir in drained clams. Chill. At serving time, thin with cream to dipping consistency.

11
Shrimp Cheese Dip

2 lbs. boiled shrimp
1 8 oz. pkg. cream cheese
Juice of one lemon
10 green onions
Mayonnaise, hot sauce, salt, pepper or other seasonings

Mix softened cheese with juice. Chop shrimp and mince onions. Add to cheese. Add mayonnaise until mixture is of dipping consistency. Add seasonings to taste. Let stand 8 hrs. before serving.

12
Cheese Puff Snacks

1/2 C butter
8 eggs
3/4 C flour
1 t baking powder
2 C small curd cottage cheese
3 C shredded swiss or Monterey
  Jack cheese

Melt butter in oven in a 12 x 8 baking dish. Beat eggs until foamy and add rest of ingredients. Pour mixture over melted butter and stir until butter is combined. Bake 35-40 minutes at 400 degrees. Cut in bite-sized pieces. Can also be served hot in larger squares, plain or with a cream sauce for a main dish. 20-25 bite-sized pieces.

Cheese changes plain recipes into gourmet food

13
Holiday Appetizer
Some red and green even

1 8 oz. pkg. cream cheese
2 T milk
3/4 C dried beef, chopped
2 T instant minced onion
2 t minced green pepper
1/8 t black pepper
1/2 C sour cream
1/4 C chopped nuts

Mix all ingredients and bake at 350 degrees, 15 minutes, or heat until hot in microwave. Serve hot or cold with crackers and chips.

14
Cheese Olive Balls

1 C grated medium cheddar cheese
1/2 C flour
2 T butter
Stuffed olives

Mix cheese, flour and butter to make a dough. Break off small pieces and flatten in hand. Wrap olive in dough. Bake until golden brown in 375-400 degrees, about 12 minutes.

15

Pepper Cheese Appetizer
Hot pepper lovers love this

Jalapeno peppers, fresh or canned
1 lb. cheddar cheese,
  cut in thick slices
4 eggs
1 lb. Monterey Jack cheese,
  cut in thick slices

Grease a 9 x 12 baking dish. Slice peppers in a layer in pan, using amount desired for taste. Cover peppers with sliced cheddar. Beat eggs and pour over cheese. Finish with sliced Monterey Jack. Sprinkle with parsley, if desired. Bake 35 minutes at 350 degrees. Cut in 1" squares.

16

Cheese Straws
A holiday treat

1½ C flour
6 T shortening
5 T ice water
1/2 t salt
1 C grated Parmesan
dash each, paprika, cayenne pepper and tobasco sauce

Mix flour, salt, cheese and seasonings. Cut in shortening and add water mixing with a fork. Place dough in cookie press and use star form. Form dough in long lines on a cookie sheet, cut in desired lengths. Bake at 400 degrees, 5-10 minutes.

17
Crab and Cheese Cracker Spread

8 oz. cream cheese
1 can crabmeat
1 T horseradish
5 T catsup

Soften cheese and spread on a dinner plate. Sprinkle crabmeat over cheese. Mix catsup and horseradish, and spread over all. Serve with crackers.

18
Cracker Spread

1 lb. process cheese
1/3 C horseradish
1 C mayonnaise

Melt ingredients in a double boiler. Pour into serving container and let set. Spread on crackers.

Americans were the first to make process cheese. It was the first new development in cheesemaking in hundreds of years

19

Cheese Asparagus Canapes

20 slices sandwich bread
8 oz. cream cheese
4 oz. blue cheese
1 egg
20 spears canned asparagus
1/2 lb. melted butter

Trim crusts from bread. Mix egg with cheeses and spread on bread slices. Roll one asparagus spear in each slice, and roll slices in melted butter. Place rolls on a cookie sheet and freeze. At serving time, slice each roll in three pieces and bake at 400 degrees, 15 minutes, or until slightly brown.

20

Crab or Shrimp Canapes

1 pkg. frozen crab or shrimp
1¼ C grated Swiss cheese
1/2 C mayonnaise
1/4 t curry powder
1 t lemon juice
Salt and pepper
1 T minced onion
Melba toast rounds

Combine all ingredients and spread on toast rounds. Bake 8-10 minutes at 400 degrees. These may be frozen and stored. Reheat before serving.

21

Blue Cheese Dip
Low in calories, great for veggies

2 T milk
1/2 t Worcestershire
12 oz. cream style cottage cheese
2½ oz. blue cheese
2 T chopped onion
1/8 t monosodium glutamate

Put all ingredients in blender and blend until smooth. Refrigerate for 2 hours before serving.

Plan on 1-2 ounces of dip per person

22

Cheese and Crab Dip
The best!

1 6½ oz. can crabmeat
12 oz. cream cheese
3 T mayonnaise
1/4 t salt
1/8 t curry powder
1 T grated onion
1½ T lemon juice
1/2 t Worcestershire sauce

Crumble crabmeat, add to softened cheese. Add rest of ingredients and chill.

23

Beer Cheese Crackers

2 C biscuit mix
1/2 C shredded cheddar
1/2 C beer
2 T butter, melted
Sesame or poppy seeds

Mix biscuit mix, beer and cheese. Beat well. Form into a ball and knead 5 times. Roll into rectangle 16 x 10 inches. Cut in 2" squares, then cut each square in half diagonally. Brush with melted butter and sprinkle with seeds. Bake on an ungreased baking sheet at 450 degrees, about 8 minutes or until golden.

24

Cheddar Rice Crackers

1/2 C margarine
1 C flour
1/2 t baking powder
2 C shredded sharp cheese
2 C crisp rice cereal
1/2 t salt

Blend flour, margarine, baking powder and salt. Add cheese and cereal. Shape into walnut-sized balls, and flatten slightly on ungreased baking sheet. Bake at 350 degrees, 12 minutes. 4-5 dozen.

SALADS

Family Cheese Favorites

25

Cottage Cheese Fruit Mold

1 envelope unflavored gelatin
1/4 C water
2 T lemon juice
1/4 t salt
1 C whipping cream or whipped
  topping
2 C cream style cottage cheese
3 C mixed fresh fruit
  (peaches, grapes, apple, etc.)

Soften gelatin in water. In saucepan, heat gelatin, lemon juice, and salt. Heat until dissolved. Whip cream, and combine with cottage cheese, and cooled gelatin. Pour mixture into oiled mold and chill until set. Unmold and fill center, or surround mold with fresh fruit. Serves 8.

Cottage cheeese is a soft, uncured cheese.

26

7-Up Salad

8 oz. cream cheese
1 3 oz. pkg. lemon gelatin
1 3 oz. pkg. lime gelatin
2 C hot water
1 #2 can crushed pineapple
1 8 oz. bottle 7-Up
1 t sugar
1 t vanilla

Drain pineapple and cream softened cheese with the juice. Dissolve gelatin in hot water, cool and add gradually to cheese. Add remaining ingredi-ents and set. Serves 8.

27

Quick Cottage Salad
*Make it in a minute,
any color or flavor.*

1 lb. small curd creamed
   cottage cheese
1 large pkg. flavored gelatin
1 lg. container whipped topping
1 #2 can crushed pineapple
   and juice

Mix dry gelatin into cheese. Add fruit and juice. Fold in whipped topping. Put mixture in serving dish and garnish with fruit as desired. Chill. Serves 8-10.

Spinach Cottage Cheese Salad
A green and white treat for a crowd.

1 lb. fresh spinach
1 large head lettuce
4-5 slices bacon
1/4 C sugar
1½ C cottage cheese
1 T minced onion
1 C salad oil
1/3 C vinegar
1 t salt
1 t dry mustard

Clean spinach and tear out stems. Mix with lettuce torn in bite-sized pieces. Fry bacon until crisp and add to greens. Mix sugar, onion, oil, vinegar, salt and mustard. Beat well. Add half of dressing to greens and the rest to the cottage cheese. Chill. Add cheese mixture just before serving. Serves 12.

Peachy Cheese Party Salad
An unusual combination.

2 pkgs. orange gelatin
2 C boiling water
1 30 oz. can crushed pineapple
2 C fresh or frozen peaches
1/2 C sugar
3 T flour
1 egg
3 T butter
1 C miniature marshmallows
1½ C shredded sharp cheese
1 C whipped cream or topping

Dissolve gelatin in boiling water. Drain pineapple and add water to juice to make 1½ C liquid. Add 3/4 C of juice to gelatin. Spread peaches over bottom of 13 x 9 inch pan and pour gelatin over fruit. Chill until set. Combine sugar, flour and remaining juice. Cook until thickened, stir in butter and chill. Fold remaining ingredients into chilled mixture, reserving 1/2 C cheese. Spread mixture over gelatin, sprinkle with reserved cheese and chill overnight. Serves 16.

30
Cottage Cheese Apricot Salad

2 pkg. lemon gelatin
1 C hot water
1 C apricot nectar
1 C apricots, sliced
1/2 C Maraschino cherries
1 C cottage cheese
1/2 C nutmeats
1 C whipped cream or whipped topping

Soften gelatin in hot water, add apricot nectar, and chill until thickened. Mix in fruits, cheese and nuts. Fold in whipped topping. Chill until set.

31
Broccoli-Raisin Cheese Salad
Attractive, unusual and delicious!

1/2 head raw broccoli
1/3 C raisins
1/2 C bacon bits
3/4 C shredded cheese
2 T onion, diced
1/2 C salad dressing
1 T vinegar
2 T sugar

Cut broccoli in bite-sized pieces. Add raisins, bacon, onions and cheese. Toss with dressing and chill 2 hours before serving. Serves 6.

32

Apple-Cheese Salad
Pretty and good.

1 C boiling water
3 T red cinnamon candies
1 3 oz. pkg. lemon gelatin
1½ C sweetened applesauce
1 8 oz. pkg. cream cheese
1/2 C nuts, chopped
1/2 C celery, diced
1/2 C mayonnaise

Pour boiling water over candies, stir to dissolve. Add gelatin, stir until completely dissolved. Add applesauce. Pour half of mixture in 8 x 8 x 2″ serving dish. Chill. Blend cheese, nuts, celery and mayonnaise. Spred in layer over firm apple mixture. Pour on remaining apple mixture. Chill until firm. 6 servings.

33

Cottage Vegetable Salad

1 pkg. lime gelatin
1 C boiling water
1/2 C chopped celery
1/4 C green pepper
1 T pimento
3-4 green onions
1/3 C evaporated milk
1/2 C salad dressing
1 C cottage cheese

Dissolve gelatin in boiling water. Add finely chopped vegetables, using the onion tops also. Blend in salad dressing and cheese. Whip chilled evaporated milk and stir in. Turn into an oiled mold and set. Serves 6

34

Cheese Cucumber Salad
A dieter's delight!

1 3 oz. pkg. lemon gelatin
1/2 C hot water
1 lb. cottage cheese
1 C salad dressing
1 t vinegar
1 small onion
1 medium cucumber

Mince unpeeled cucumber. Mince onion. Mix these two ingredients with cheese, salad dressing and vinegar. Dissolve gelatin in boiling water and stir immediately into first mixture. Let set. Serves 6.

35

7 Layer Salad
Use other combinations that you like.
The apple and onion are super together!
Serves a big crowd.

1 small head lettuce
1 C chopped sweet onion
1 C chopped green pepper
1 C diced unpeeled apple
1 C mayonnaise
1 C crisp bacon, crumbled
1 C shredded cheddar cheese

Break lettuce into 13 x 9″ pan. Sprinkle with desired amount of onion and pepper. Dice apple into salt water, drain and sprinkle on salad. With a spatula, spread on mayonnaise in a 1/4 inch layer. Sprinkle with 2 T sugar. (Use no salt). Top with crisp bacon pieces and shredded cheese. Cover and chill 4-6 hours or overnight. Keeps very well for a day or two.

Cheese Macaroni Salad

2 C uncooked macaroni
1/2 C diced sharp Cheddar
1/2 C diced sharp Pinconning
1/2 C diced medium Colby
1/2 C sweet pickle relish
2/3 C sliced green olives
1/2 C diced purple onion

3/4-1- C Thousand Island dressing

Cook macaroni just until tender, drain and put in large bowl. Add remaining ingredients and toss with dressing. Chill. Toss again before serving. Let warm to room temperature to improve flavor. Garnish with hard-cooked egg wedges, tomato wedges and black olives. Serves 6.

The art of cheesemaking is thought to have been discovered in Asia more than 4000 years ago.

37

Cheese Salad
For sandwiches

1/2 lb. medium cheddar
1/2 lb. Pinconning sharp
1 C salad dressing
1/2 C sour cream
2 T sugar
2 T mustard
1/4 C milk
1 T vinegar
1 T horseradish
2 T minced onion

Shred or grind cheeses and mix with rest of ingredients. Makes 12 sandwiches.

38

Cheese ' N Egg Sandwich Spread
Good on crackers and rye bread

1 1/2 lb. medium cheddar
8-10 large sweet pickles
1 oz. pimentos (save juice)
2 small onions
6 hard boiled eggs
1 C salad dressing (or more)

Grind or put through food processor cheese, pickles, pimentos, onions and eggs. Mix pimento juice with dressing, and add to cheese mixture until of spreading consistency. Keeps well in refrigerator up to two weeks.

39
Taco Salad

A main dish salad.

1 lb. ground beef
1 C chili hot beans
1 small head lettuce
1 medium green pepper
1 small onion
1 med. tomato
2 C shredded cheese
1-2 C crumbled tortilla chips

Dressing:
1 pkg. taco seasoning mix
1 C mayonnaise
1 C buttermilk

Cook beef and drain excess fat. Add beans and heat through. Chop onion, pepper and tomato. Toss with broken lettuce and cheese. Just before serving, add dressing and sprinkle with taco chips. Serves 8.

40
Cheese and Ham Salad

Dressing:
1/4 C mayonnaise
1/2 C sour cream
1/2 t prepared mustard
1/2 t curry powder
1 T lemon juice
1/2 t finely chopped onion
Dash cayenne pepper

4 medium tomatoes or may use
 cherry tomatoes
1 C cooked, cubed ham
1 C cubed Havarti cheese or
 cheese of choice
1 C diced celery
1/2 green pepper, chopped

Cut tomatoes in bite-sized pieces, drain extra juice and mix with rest of salad ingredients. Combine dressing ingredients and add to salad. Refrigerate 2 hours. Serve with crusty french bread. Serves 6.

41
Blue Cheese Yogurt Dressing

1/3 C blue cheese
1/3 C mayonnaise
1 C plain yogurt

Mix cheese and mayonnaise, fold in yogurt.

For Salads or Sandwiches

42
Bleu Cheese Salad Dressing

2 C sour cream
1 C mayonnaise
1 T lemon juice
1 t garlic salt
4 oz. crumbled bleu cheese

Mix altogether. Refrigerate. Keeps well.

Roquefort cheese gets its blue-veined appearance and sharp flavor from penicillin mold.

Family Cheese Favorites

SOUPS &
SANDWICHES

Family Cheese Favorites

Beer Cheese Soup
Very good flavor

1 C diced carrots
1 C diced celery
1 C chopped onion
2 T oil
3 C chicken broth
1 C sharp cheddar
4 T flour
1/2 t dry mustard
1/8 t hot sauce, if desired
1/2 t Worcestershire sauce
1 12 oz. can beer
1/2 lb sliced sausage

In heavy soup pan, cook vegetables in oil until tender crisp. Add broth and simmer for 45 minutes. Mix cubed or grated cheese with flour and stir gradually into soup, stirring constantly. Add sausage and seasonings and simmer 15 minutes. Add beer, stir well and serve. Serves 8.

44

Hearty Cheese Soup

5 T butter
2 carrots
2 ribs celery
1 medium onion
1/2 green pepper
4-5 large mushrooms
1/2 C cooked ham
1/2 C flour
2 T cornstarch
1 qt chicken broth
1 qt milk
1/2 t paprika
1/2 t cayenne
1/2 t dry mustard
1 lb sharp cheese
Salt and pepper to taste

In a heavy Dutch oven, melt butter and cook diced vegetables and ham for 10 minutes over medium heat. Do not brown. Add flour and cornstarch stirring constantly. Add broth and stir until slightly thickened. Add milk and seasonings, then add cheese that has been diced or grated and stir constantly until cheese is melted. Do not boil after adding cheese! Season to taste and serve very hot. Serves 8-10.

45

Soup with Cheese Dumplings
Loved by children and adults alike

2 C flour
3 t baking powder
1/2 t salt
3 T shortening
3/4 C milk
1/2 lb American cheese
2 cans Cream of Tomato soup
1/2 C water

Combine flour, baking powder and salt. Cut in shortening. Add milk gradually, stirring with fork until a soft biscuit dough is formed. Cut cheese in 1/2 inch cubes. Break off balls of dough and wrap cheese cubes in dough, sealing completely. Combine soup with water and bring to a boil. Drop cheese balls in soup. Cover pan and cook slowly for 15-20 minutes. (do not lift lid) Ladle the soup with dumplings into serving dishes. 6 servings.

46

Cream Cheese Soup
White, creamy and delicious

2 C water
1 C chopped carrot
1/2 C chopped onion
1/2 C chopped celery
1 t salt
Dash hot pepper sauce
8 oz. cream cheese
2 C milk
2 T butter
2 T flour

Cook vegetables in water until tender. Add cream cheese, cut in chunks. Add milk. Stir until cheese is melted. Mix flour and butter. Add to hot soup and stir until thickened. Serve hot with a sprinkle of dried parsley.

An ounce of cream cheese contains about 100 calories

47

Easy Broccoli & Cheese Soup
A hot treat in a hurry

2 cans cream of mushroom soup
1 bunch broccoli, steamed until
 tender, or 1 10 oz. pkg. frozen
 broccoli cooked and chopped.
3/4 C cheddar cheese
1½ C water
1/2 C milk
Salt and pepper to taste

Mix soup, milk and water, heat until hot, but not boiling. Add broccoli and cheese, stirring until cheese is melted. Cook on low for 5 minutes, stirring to avoid scorching.

Cheddar cheese is usually cured from 60 days to 2 years.

48

Cheddar Cheese Soup
Medium thick and rich

1 stick butter or oleo
1½ C diced celery
1 C diced carrot
1/2 C chopped onion
1/2 C flour
3/4 t paprika
8 C chicken stock
1 qt half & half
1/2 lb sharp cheddar, diced
1½ t Worcestershire
Yellow food coloring, and salt
 if desired

In a heavy saucepan cook vegetables in butter until soft. Add flour and paprika, stirring until bubbly. Add chicken stock, stirring until smooth. Simmer, covered 1 hour. Add cheese, half & half and Worcestershire. Continue cooking and stirring until cheese is melted and mixture is heated through. Add salt and food coloring as desired. Serves 12.

49
Corned Beef Picnic Buns
Keep these in the freezer to pop into a picnic basket

1 can corned beef
1 C sharp cheese, shredded
2 T chopped green pepper
1/4 C chopped onion
2 T Worcestershire sauce
1/2 C chopped ripe olives
1/2 C catsup

Mix altogether and spread on 8 buns. Wrap in foil. Heat 20 minutes at 350 degrees. May freeze before baking, but thaw before heating.

50
Hot Tuna Cheese Buns

1 can tuna
1 C. diced chedder cheese
3 hard boiled eggs
2 T diced green pepper
2 T chopped onion
2 T chopped green olives
2 T pickle relish
1/2 C salad dressing

Mix together and fill 12 buns with mixture. Wrap sandwiches in foil and heat in oven, 30 minutes, 250 degrees.

51
Patio Poor Boys

3 large hard rolls
1/4 C melted butter
4 hard cooked eggs, chopped
1/4 C chopped green pepper
1/4 C chopped stuffed olives
2 chopped green onions
1/2 C sharp cheese, cubed
1/4 C chili sauce
1/2 t salt
1/4 t chili powder
Pepper to taste

Split rolls and hollow out insides to make sandwich shell. Brush shells with melted butter. Combine all ingredients and heap mixture in shells. Bake at 400 degrees, 15 minutes or until cheese is melted and rolls slightly brown and crisp. 6 sandwiches.

You can cut about 50 ¾ inch cheese cubes from one pound.

52

Baked Asparagus Cheese Sandwiches

6 thick slices firm bread
6 slices Swiss cheese
4 eggs
2 C milk
1 t salt
1/8 t pepper
1/4 t nutmeg
1 T minced onion
18 cooked asparagus spears
1/2 C shredded cheddar

Trim bread crusts and arrange slices in 9 x 13 baking pan. Top each bread slice with Swiss cheese. Beat eggs and add milk, seasonings and onion. Pour over bread. Bake 25 minutes at 325 degrees. Remove from oven and top each slice with three asparagus spears. Sprinkle with cheese. Return to oven and bake 10-15 minutes until custard sets and tops are golden. Let stand 5 minutes before serving. 6 servings.

Pizza Burgers

A favorite of hungry teens

1½ lbs ground beef
1 10½ oz.can pizza sauce
1/4 C sliced green onions
1/3 C Parmesan cheese
1 loaf French bread
Sliced tomatoes
8-10 slices American cheese

Brown meat and pour off excess fat. Mix pizza sauce into meat. Slice bread lengthwise, butter lightly and toast in broiler. Remove from boiler and spread with meat. Sprinkle with Parmesan. Place thin tomato slices overlapping on loaves. Top with overlapping cheese slices. Heat in 400 degree oven until hot and cheese is melted. Serves 8.

Nutrition experts classify cheese as a complete protein food

Pizza Treats
For the "after the game" crowd.

3 lb. ground beef
1/2 lb. longhorn cheese
1/2 lb. Mozzarella
1½ t salt
1 ½ t sage
1 T oregano
2 T parsley flakes
3½ C tomato sauce
1 dozen English muffins

Reserve 2 cups shredded cheese. Brown meat and drain excess fat. Mix remaining cheese and rest of ingredients into meat. Simmer 30 minutes. Spoon on muffin halves and sprinkle with reserved cheese. Bake 10 minutes at 350 degrees.

Shredding cheese is easy when cheese is very cold

Long Long Sandwich
Make ahead and serve a crowd

1 loaf french bread
1/4 C butter
2 T prepared mustard
2 Cans deviled ham
1 C shredded cheddar
1/4 C minced onion
Thin dill pickles slices

Slice bread vertically in 3/4 inch slices, down to, but not through bottom crust. Mix butter and mustard, butter bread slices. Spread ham between every other slice and shredded cheese between alternate slices. Spoon onion over ham, insert pickles into cheese slices. Wrap in foil and heat at 400 degrees 12-15 minutes until bread is hot and cheese melted. Slice in 1½ inch slices.

An ounce of cheddar cheese contains about 114 calories.

Breads & Rolls

Family Cheese Favorites

56
Spinach Cheese Bread

1 loaf frozen bread dough
3 oz. cream cheese
9 oz. pkg. frozen spinach
1/2 C cottage cheese
1 egg
2 C shredded Feta cheese
1/2 t white pepper
1/4 t garlic powder
Egg wash, sesame seed

Thaw bread and place on greased cookie sheet. Press to form a 15 x 12 inch rectangle. Spread with cream cheese. Thaw spinach and squeeze out liquid. Place spinach in a 4 inch strip down center of dough to within one inch of ends. Combine cheeses, garlic and pepper. Spread over spinach. Fold ends of loaf in, fold long side over filling, overlapping a little. Seal well. Brush with beaten egg, sprinkle with seasame seed. Bake 25-30 minutes at 375 degrees. Let stand 5 minutes before slicing. Serves 6.

57

Cheese Pimento Bread

2 T soft butter
3 T flour
1 T sugar
2 t salt
1¼ C milk
1/3 C grated sharp cheese
2-3 T chopped pimiento
1/4 C warm water
1 pkg. yeast
3-3½ C flour

Combine butter, 2 T flour, sugar and salt, add milk and cook until thickened. Add cheese and pimiento. Cool to lukewarm. Soften yeast in water and add to milk mixture. Stir in flour and knead well. Let rise until double in bulk, punch down and let rise again. Shape into loaf and place in greased loaf pan. Let rise. Bake 35-40 minutes at 375 degrees. 1 loaf.

58
Cheese Buns

1 pkg. dry yeast
1/4 C warm water
1 T sugar
1 C grated cheese
1¼ C warm milk
4 C flour
1 t salt

Soften yeast in water, add sugar. Melt cheese in milk. Add yeast and 1 C flour. Beat well and let rise for 1 hour. Add salt and remaining flour. Knead lightly. Let rise until double. Knead again for 2 minutes and shape into buns. Place on greased baking sheet and let rise until light. Bake at 400 degrees, 12-15 minutes. Butter tops of rolls.

59
Cream Cheese Bread

2¼ C flour
1-1/3 C sugar
1 t salt
1 T baking powder
1/2 C shortening
2 eggs
1 C milk
1 8 oz. pkg. cream cheese
1/2 C chopped walnuts
2 T grated orange rind

Glaze:
1/4 C orange juice
1/3 C sugar

Cream shortening and sugar. Blend in eggs, beating well. Add dry ingredients alternately with milk. Cut cheese in 1/2 inch cubes and fold into batter, along with nuts and rind. Pour into two greased and floured loaf pans. Bake at 325 degrees, 60 minutes. Combine sugar and juice and pour over hot loaves. Store in refrigerator for easy slicing.

60

Cheese Bread
3 loaves.. Just try it for toast!

1¾ C scalded milk
3 C shredded process cheese
4 T sugar
2 t salt
1 pkg. dry yeast
1/4 C warm water
5½ C flour

Put 2 C cheese, sugar, salt and butter into hot milk an stir until cheese melts. Soften yeast in warm water and add to milk mixture. Add 5 C flour, 1 C cheese and mix well. Turn out on floured board and knead until smooth. Place dough in a large bowl, butter top, cover and let rise about 1½ hours until doubled in bulk. Punch down, divide in thirds and place loaves in greased loaf pans. Cover and let rise until doubled. Bake 30-45 minutes at 375 degrees. Remove from pans and cool.

61
Corny Cheese Cornbread

1½ C yellow cornmeal
1 T baking powder
1/2 t salt
2 eggs
1/2 C shortening
1/2 C chopped onion
1 C sour cream
1 8-10 oz. can creamed style corn
1 C grated sharp cheese
1/4-1/2 C chopped Jalepeno peppers, if desired

Cream shortening, eggs and sour cream. Add rest of ingredients and mix just until blended. Fill 12 greased muffin cups, or (1) 10 inch greased baking pan. Bake at 400 degrees, 20 minutes for muffins, 30-40 minutes for pan. 8-12 servings.

62

Cottage Cheese Bread

Cut in wedges, serve with a salad for lunch.

1 pkg. dry yeast
1/2 C warm water
1/2 C cottage cheese
1 T butter 1 egg
1/3 C finely chopped onion
1 T sugar
1 T dill seed
1 T salt
3/4 t baking soda
1/2 C wheat germ
1¾-2 C flour

Soften yeast in water. Heat cottage cheese and butter until lukewarm. Add egg, onion, sugar, dill seed, salt, and soda. Mix well and stir in yeast. Add wheat gem and flour gradually to make a stiff dough. Cover and let rise until double. Knead for one minute on a floured board. Pat dough into a greased 9 inch cake pan or other 2 inch deep baking dish. Let rise again until double. Bake at 350 degrees, 25-30 minutes. Serve warm. 6 servings.

63
Cheese Jam Braid

1 3 oz. pkg. cream cheese
1/4 C butter
2 C biscuit mix
1/3 C milk
1/2 C jam (raspberry,
strawberry, peach)

Cut cheese and butter into biscuit mix until crumbly. Stir in milk and turn onto floured board. Knead a few times. Pat dough to an 8 x 10 inch rectangle on a sheet of waxed paper. Turn onto a greased baking sheet and remove paper. Spread jam on center third of dough. Cut outside thirds in strips and fold to center in a braid. Bake at 425 degrees, 12-15 minutes. Cool and drizzle with powdered sugar icing.

64

Cheese-Blueberry Muffins

1½ C flour
1 C yellow cornmeal
1/2 C sugar
3 t baking powder
1 t salt
2 C shredded sharp cheddar
2 C fresh or frozen blueberries
1 C milk
1 egg
1/4 C melted butter

Combine dry ingredients and carefully stir in cheese and berries. Combine milk, egg and butter. Mix well. Stir milk mixture into dry ingredients just until moistened. Spoon into greased muffin tins. Bake at 400 degrees, 20-25 minutes. 18-20 muffins.

65
Cheddar Muffins

2 C flour
2 oz. grated cheddar
1 T dried parsley
1 T baking powder
3/4 t salt
3 T sugar
1 egg
1 C sour cream
1/2 C milk
1/4 C melted butter

In a bowl combine dry ingredients and cheese. In another bowl, mix remaining ingredients. Pour the liquids into the flour-cheese mixture and stir just until blended. Spoon into greased muffin cups. Bake at 400 degrees, 20-25 minutes. 12 large muffins.

Mold is not harmful on cheese. Just scrape it off and use as usual

MAIN DISHES

Family Cheese Favorites

66

Corned Beef and Cheese Casserole

1 8 oz. pkg. noodles
1 can corned beef 1 can cream of mushroom soup
1 C milk
1/2 C chopped onion
1 C cubed sharp cheese

Cook noodles just until tender in salted water. Mix with beef, which has been broken into small pieces, and mix in rest of ingredients. Place mixture in a greased 2 qt. casserole. Top with cracker crumbs. Bake at 350 degrees, 45 minutes. Serves 8.

67

Broccoli Ham & Cheese

Quick and delicious.

2 pkg. frozen broccoli
2 C cubed ham
1½ C cubed medium cheese
1 C biscuit mix
2½ C milk
4 eggs

Put thawed broccoli in bottom of greased 8 x 8 baking pan. Top with ham and cheese. Mix biscuit mix, milk and eggs and pour over ingredients in pan. Bake at 350 degrees, 1 hour uncovered.

68
Irish Cheese and Potato Pie

1 C milk
1 C cheddar cheese, cubed
1 t Worcestershire sauce
1/2 t salt
Pepper
1 T flour
3 medium raw potatoes, sliced
2 C sliced onion
3 T butter
2 T dry bread crumbs

Combine milk and cheese and heat in heavy pan until cheese melts. Add Worcestershire. In a greased 9 inch pie pan place 1/2 of potatoes, sprinkle with 1/2 of flour, mixed with salt and pepper. Add 1/2 of onions, dot with butter, and repeat layers, using remaining ingredients. Pour cheese sauce over all, top with bread crumbs and bake at 350 degrees, 45 minutes. Serves 4.

It takes about 11 pounds of milk to make one pound of cheese

69

Cheese-Mushroom-Tomato Bake
Super vegetarian luncheon dish.

2 7 oz. pkgs. Gouda cheese
1/2 C melted butter
4 slices bread, crumbled
2 large tomatoes
1 lb. fresh mushrooms

Shred 2 C of cheese and cut the rest in slices. Mix 1½ C shredded cheese, butter and crumbs. Press into a greased 8 x 12 inch baking dish. Cover bottom with cheese slices. Add a layer of tomato slices. Saute mushrooms (or may use 8 oz. canned mushrooms) and spread over tomatoes. Sprinkle with remaining shredded cheese. Bake at 350 degrees, 20 minutes. Serves 6.

Choosing cheese is like choosing a friend. It takes time and care.

70
Salmon Cheese Puff

3/4 C chopped onion
1/2 C chopped green pepper
1/4 C butter
1 can cream of celery soup
1 C milk
2 eggs, separated
1 1# can salmon
1 C shredded cheese
1 T lemon juice
2 C soft bread crumbs

Cook onion and pepper in butter until golden. Add soup and milk, and bring to a boil. Add a little of the hot mixture to slightly beaten egg yolks, and add back to hot mixture. Cook one minute. Add rest of ingredients, except for egg whites and mix well. Beat egg whites until stiff and fold into mixture. Place in a greased 1½ qt. casserole, bake at 350 degrees, 30-35 minutes. Serves 6.

71

Cheese and Ham Supper Loaf
Leftover ham was never this good before!

1 C cubed ham
1 C cubed mild cheese
1 C cubed swiss cheese
6 eggs
6 slices bacon
3/4 C milk
1½ C flour
2½ t baking powder
1/2 t salt

Fry bacon until crisp, drain and crumble. Beat eggs, add milk, flour, baking powder and salt. Beat until smooth. Add remaining ingredients. Pour into greased loaf pan and bake 50-60 minutes at 350 degrees. Slice and serve hot. 8 servings.

An ounce of Swiss cheese contains about 105 calories.

72

Cheese Broccoli Custard

6 eggs
2 lbs. small curd
  cottage cheese
6 T flour
1/2 lb. diced sharp cheddar
2 pkg. frozen chopped
  broccoli
1 stick butter or margarine
2 green onions, chopped
Salt and pepper

Have all ingredients at room temperature. Mix well with electric mixer. Turn into a greased 2 qt. casserole. Bake 1 hour at 350 degrees. Serves 8.

73

Cream Cheese Fondue

16 oz. cream cheese
2 C milk
1½ C grated Parmesan cheese
1 t garlic salt
1/4 t pepper

Melt cream cheese and milk in double boiler. Add remaining ingredients and pour in fondue pot. Use crusty french bread for dipping.

Brunch For A Bunch
Make ahead for a no-work breakfast.

6 slices white bread, cubed
1 lb. cubed ham, bacon
  or sausage
1/2 lb. Colby cheese shredded
2 T green pepper (if desired)
3-4 eggs
2 C milk
1/2 t dry mustard
1/2 t salt
1/4 C melted butter
1 4 oz. can mushrooms

Layer bread, meat, cheese and mushrooms in a 9 x 13 inch baking pan. Beat eggs, add milk and seasonings. Pour evenly over layered mixture. Pour melted butter on top. Sprinkle with green pepper, or may use paprika. Cover tightly and refrigerate overnight. Uncover. Bake at 325 degrees, 1 hour. Serves 8.

75

Escalloped Cheese

6-8 slices whole wheat bread
4 T soft butter
8 oz. medium cheddar, sliced
2 eggs
1 C milk
1 t salt

Lightly butter bread and cut into cubes. In a greased casserole dish layer bread cubes and cheese slices to make four layers. Beat eggs, add milk and salt. Pour over cheese and bread. Bake at 350 degrees, 20 minutes. Serves 6.

76

Cheese Potato Casserole

2 lb. frozen hash brown potatoes
8 cups
2 cans cream of potato soup
1 C sour cream
8 oz. shredded sharp cheese

Thaw potatoes. Mix all ingredients, place in a 9 x 12 baking dish. Cover and refrigerate overnight. Sprinkle top with paprika and parsley flakes. Bake at 350 degrees, 1½ hrs. Serves 12.

Cheezy Spinach Loaf

2 C cooked spinach
2 eggs
3/4 C Parmesan cheese
2 T bacon drippings
1 C cracker crumbs
1 T vinegar

Mix and bake in greased loaf pan, 350 degrees, 30 minutes. Serve with sauce.

Sauce:
Cut 4 slices bacon in small pieces and saute with 1/4 C chopped onion. Add 1 C chopped tomato, 1/4 C chopped green pepper, salt and pepper to taste. Thicken to desired consistency with cornstarch mixed with water.

Cheeses are like people. Some have more personality than others.

78

Cheese Mushroom Casserole

6 slices stale bread
1/2 C celery, chopped
1/2 C onion, chopped
1/2 C green pepper, chopped
1/2 C mayonnaise
1½ C sliced fresh mushrooms
3/4 C milk
1 egg
1 can cream of mushroom
  soup
1/2 lb. shredded sharp cheddar

Butter bread and cut in cubes. Butter 1½ qt. casserole dish. Place 1/2 of bread cubes in dish, add celery, onions, and spread with mayonnaise. Saute mushrooms and add to mixture in dish. Mix milk with egg and pour over mushrooms. Add rest of bread cubes, cover and refrigerate overnight. When ready to bake, spread mushroom soup on top of casserole, and sprinkle with cheese. Bake uncovered 60 minutes, at 350 degrees. Serves 6-8.

Cheese-Zucchini Casserole
Smells good, looks good, tastes good.

1 C medium cheddar, cubed
1 C cooked brown rice
2 lbs. thinly sliced zucchini
1/2 C sliced green onion
1 t salt
1/2 t garlic powder
1 t dried sweet basil
2 beaten eggs

Mix all ingredients together lightly. Place in oiled casserole dish. Bake at 350 degrees, 1 hour. Serves 6. (Meat may be added: browned ground beef or polish sausage slices.)

Cheese keeps its perfect condition when wrapped in foil or plastic wrap and stored in the refrigerator in an airtight container

80

Pasta with Vegetables and Cheese
A vegetarian treat.

1 16 oz. pkg. frozen broccoli,
  cauliflower and carrots
16 oz. container Ricotta cheese
8 oz. linguini
1/2 C sour cream
3/4 C milk
1/2 C Parmesan cheese
1/4 t basil
1/2 t oregano
1/4 t garlic salt

Cook vegetables as directed, using salted water. Cook linguini as directed. Combine remaining ingredients and heat, but do not boil. Toss hot, drained vegetables with hot, drained pasta. Add the cheese mixture and serve immediately. 4-6 servings.

Cheese is often named for the town where it is made, thus the same cheese can have many different names

81
Cheese Tortillas
Easy, for a crowd.

1/3 C oil
1 pkg. corn tortillas
1 C finely chopped green pepper
1/2 C chopped green olives
1/2 C chopped green onion
2 C shredded cheddar cheese

Cut tortillas in half and fry, a few at a time until crisp in hot oil. Drain on paper towels. Place tortillas on a baking sheet. Mix vegetables and spoon onto shells. Sprinkle with cheese. Broil 1-2 minutes until cheese melts. Serve immediately. 6 servings.

82
Cheese Meat Loaf

2 lbs. ground beef
1/4 C chopped green pepper
3/4 C chopped onion
2 eggs
1 C diced sharp cheese
2 C soft bread crumbs
1½ C tomato juice
2 t salt
1/4 t thyme

Combine all ingredients and mix well with hands. Place in a 9 x 5 x 3″ loaf pan. Bake at 350 degrees, 1¼ hours. Let stand in pan 5 minutes and drain off excess liquid. Serves 8.

83

Taco Pie
A super luncheon dish.

Crust:
3/4 C corn meal
1/2 t salt
1/2 C flour
1/3 C butter or margarine
4 T water

Mix ingredients, roll out crust to
fit 9 inch pie pan. Chill.

Filling:
1 lb. ground beef
1/2 C chopped onion
1 T chili powder
1/2 t cumin
Dash pepper
1 lb. can tomatoes and juice
2 eggs
1 T cornstarch
3/4 C shredded med-sharp cheese

Brown beef and onions. Pour off fat. Add drained tomatoes, and spices. Mix juice, eggs and corn starch. Cook until thickened. Pour into crust and top with cheese. Bake at 400 degrees, 25 minutes. Cool 5 minutes before cutting. 6 servings.

Cheese can be frozen, but results will vary. It may lose some flavor and become crumbly. If you do freeze cheese, choose small pieces, wrap airtight, and thaw slowly in refrigerator

84

Fondue with Beer or Wine

1½ C dry white wine or
  1 can beer
1 clove garlic
4 C shredded cheese
2 T cornstarch
1 T brandy
Dash white pepper,
  and nutmeg
1/4 t baking soda

Pour beer or wine in a 2-quart saucepan. Add garlic and heat until bubbles start to rise. Discard garlic. Toss cheese (try mixing creamy ·Harvarti or Harvarti or other cheeses of your choice) with cornstarch and add gradually to saucepan, stirring until melted. Add brandy and spices. Pour into fondue pot. Just before serving stir in soda.

Dippers:
French bread chunks, fresh mushrooms, celery chunks, cooked chicken, ham and shrimp pieces, apples.

85

Sharp-Cottage-Swiss Fondue

1 C creamed cottage cheese
1 C milk
2 T butter
1½ T cornstarch
1 C shredded sharp cheese
1/2 C shredded Swiss cheese
1/4 t dry mustard
1/4 t garlic powder

Mix cottage cheese and 1/4 C milk in blender until smooth. Melt butter in saucepan. Stir in cornstarch, garlic powder and dry mustard. Add 3/4 C milk and cook over medium heat, stirring constantly until thickened, about 2-3 minutes. Reduce heat, stir in cottage cheese. Add remaining cheeses and stir until melted. Transfer to fondue pot. Serves 6.

Cheese makers usually classify cheeses according to texture and flavor: Soft, medium or hard, mild, medium or sharp.

86

Quiche
A good basic recipe.

1 8-9 inch unbaked pie shell
1/2 lb. bacon, fried crisp,
  crumbled
1/2 green pepper, chopped

4 eggs
1/2 C milk
1 t flour
1 C shredded Swiss cheese
Salt
Pepper

Sprinkle bacon and pepper evenly in pie shell. Mix remaining ingredients and pour in shell. Bake at 375 degrees, 30 minutes. Let stand 5 minutes before cutting. Serves 6. May substitute ham, sausage, mushrooms, vegetables, for bacon. Also try other cheeses for variety.

87

Impossible Quiche
The crust is magic.

2 C chopped broccoli or
  cauliflower or a combination
1/2 C chopped onion
1/2 C chopped green pepper
1 C shredded cheddar cheese
1½ C milk
3/4 C biscuit mix
3 eggs
Salt
Pepper

Place vegetables and cheese in a greased 9 or 10 inch pie pan. Put milk, biscuit mix, eggs and seasonings in a blender & blend well. Pour into pan over vegetables and bake at 400 degrees, 35-40 minutes. Let stand before cutting. Serves 8.

Wisconsin is the U.S. leading cheese making state

88

Lasagna
Parmesan is all you need!

9 lasagna noodles

Meat Sauce:
1 large onion, chopped
1 clove garlic, minced
1/4 C oil
1 #2½ can tomatoes
1 can tomato paste
1½ t salt
1/4 t pepper
1/4 C water
2 lbs. lean ground beef

Cheese Sauce:
1 small onion, chopped
4 T butter
4 T flour
3/4 C Parmesan cheese
2 C milk
2 egg yolks, beaten

Saute onion and garlic in oil, add rest of ingredients except meat and mix well. Crumble raw meat in mixture. Simmer 40 minutes.

Saute onion in butter. Mix in flour and cheese. Gradually add milk and simmer until thickened. Pour a little hot sauce into egg yolks and then blend the egg mixture into sauce. Simmer 10 minutes. In a greased 9 x 13 pan, layer 3 cooked lasagna noodles, meat sauce, cheese sauce. Make 3 layers. Bake at 350 degrees, 45 minutes or until brown and bubbly. Serves 12.

Chèese provides protein for body building as well as calcium and vitamins

89

Best Ever Lasagna
Don't boil the noodles

1 lb. lean ground beef
1 C chopped onion
3 cloves minced garlic
4 C tomato juice
6 oz. tomato paste
2 C sliced fresh mushrooms
1 T Worcestershire sauce
1 t leaf oregano
1 t parsley flakes
Salt and pepper to taste
8 oz. uncooked lasagna noodles
16 oz. Ricotta cheese
1 1/2 C Parmesan and Romano
  cheese
8 oz. shredded Mozzarella cheese

Brown beef, onion and garlic, pour off excess fat and add rest of ingredients except noodles and cheeses. Simmer covered for 30 minutes. In a 13 x 9 inch pan, layer the uncooked noodles, 1/2 of sauce, 1/2 of each cheese. Repeat layers. Cover with foil and let stand 45 minutes for noodles to absorb moisture. Bake, covered at 350 degrees, 30 minutes. Uncover and bake 15 minutes more. Remove from oven and let stand 15 minutes before cutting. 8 servings.

90

Carbonara

1/2 lb. Italian bacon, or
    thick sliced bacon, or
    Canadian bacon
2 T olive oil
1 T butter
4 cloves garlic
1/4 C dry wine
3 eggs
5 T Romano cheese
2/3 C Parmesan cheese
1 lb. spaghetti
1/2 t pepper
2 T parsley

Crush garlic cloves slightly and saute in oil and butter for 3-4 minutes. Remove garlic. Cut bacon in 1/4 inch strips, add to pan and cook until slightly crisp. Remove and discard 2 T of accumulated fat. Add wine and boil for 3 minutes. Set aside. Mix eggs with the cheeses. Cook spaghetti until just tender. Drain and toss with cheese and egg mixture. Reheat bacon mixture and toss with hot spaghetti. Put into serving dish and sprinkle with pepper and parsley. Serves 8.

Enchiladas

Sauce:
2 8 oz. cans tomato paste
1/2 C margarine
1/2 C flour
2 C water
1 T chili powder
1 t vinegar
1/2 t salt
1/2 t allspice

Filling:
1 1/2 lbs. ground beef
1 large diced onions
1 1/2 t chili powder
1/2 t salt
1/4 t allspice

1 pkg. corn tortillas
1/2 lb. shredded
  American cheese

Mix chili powder with a little water and add to rest of sauce ingredients. Simmer 1 hour.

Saute meat and onion. Pour off excess fat. Add salt, allspice and chili powder. Add 1/2 of cheese to meat and cook until melted.

Dip each tortilla shell in sauce, place a spoonful of meat on shell. Roll up and fasten with toothpick. Place filled tortillas in greased 9 x 12 inch baking pan, pour remaining sauce over top, sprinkle with rest of cheese. Bake at 350 degrees, 30 minutes. Serves 8-12.

Family Cheese Favorites

Beef and Corn Au Gratin
A meal in a frypan!

2 lbs. ground beef
1/2 C chopped onion
1/2 t salt
1/4 t pepper
1 t sage
1/8 t nutmeg
2 cans whole kernel corn
8 oz. tomato sauce
1 chopped tomato
1 green pepper, sliced
2 C seasoned croutons
8 oz. cheddar cheese slices

Brown meat in frypan and drain off excess fat. Add spices and onion and cook 5 minutes. Stir in corn, tomato sauce, tomato and green pepper. Cover and simmer 10 minutes. Top with croutons and cheese slices. Heat through. Serves 6-8.

93

Chicken and Cheese

Quick, easy and delicious for company

1/4 C butter
1/4 C flour
3 chicken bouillon cubes
2 C milk
3 C cubed cooked chicken
1/2 lb. sliced mushrooms
4 C cold cooked rice
1 C grated sharp cheddar

Melt butter, blend in flour and crumbled bouillon. Gradually stir in milk, and stir until thickened. Add chicken and mushrooms to sauce. Put rice in a greased 8 x 8 baking dish, spoon chicken mixture over rice and top with cheese. Bake at 350 degrees, 30 minutes. 6 servings.

94

Spinach-Cheese Gnocchi

Italian dumplings to accompany meat dishes.
Pronounce this delicious business, "ny-oh-kee"

1 pt. Ricotta cheese
1 pkg. frozen, chopped spinach
1/4 C Parmesan cheese
1 egg
1/2 t nutmeg
1/4-1/2 C bread crumbs
Salt and pepper
Melted butter

Put Ricotta in a strainer and drain well - 3-4 hours. Cook spinach, cool and squeeze out as much liquid as possible. Mix cheese and spinach well. Add Parmesan, egg, nutmeg, salt and pepper to taste. Add bread crumbs gradually, mixing with hands, add only enough bread to allow mixture to be shaped into 1 inch balls. Roll balls in flour and place on waxed paper. Sprinkle with additional flour. Bring two quarts of salted water to a boil and drop the balls in the water, a few at a time, do not stop the boiling. After they rise to the top, boil for 3 minutes. remove with slotted spoon to serving dish. Top with melted butter and additional Parmesan. Serves 6.

Family Cheese Favorites

DESSERTS

Family Cheese Favorites

95

Lemon Cheesecake

3/4 C vanilla wafer crumbs
1 T sugar
2 T melted butter

1 pkg. lemon pudding mix
3/4 C sugar
1-1/3 C milk
3 8 oz. pkgs. cream cheese
3 eggs
1 t vanilla
Dash salt

Mix crust ingredients and sprinkle in the bottom and sides of a greased 9″ springform pan. Bring pudding mix, sugar and milk to a full boil and remove from heat. Beat cheese, eggs, vanilla and salt until smooth and add pudding. Pour in pan and bake at 425 degrees, 30 minutes. Turn off oven and open door. Leave cake in oven for 30 minutes. Cool. Serves 10-12.

96

Creamy Chocolate Cheesecake

3/4 C crushed graham crackers
2 T butter
1 T sugar

1 small pkg. chocolate pudding
3/4 C sugar
1 C milk
1 sq. unsweetened chocolate

3 oz. pkg. cream cheese
3 eggs, separated
2 t vanilla
1/4 t salt

Mix crackers, sugar and butter and sprinkle in greased 9 inch springform pan.

Bring pudding mix, sugar, milk and chocolate to a full boil, remove from heat and cover.

Beat cheese, egg yolks, vanilla and salt until smooth. Add pudding and blend. Beat egg whites and fold into cheese mixture. Pour into crumb-lined pan. Bake at 375 degrees, 35 minutes or until center is set. Cool. Serves 10-12.

97
Cream Cheese Bars

Crust:
2 C flour
2/3 C butter
1 C brown sugar
1 C chopped nuts
2 eggs
4 T milk
4 T lemon juice
1 t vanilla

Filling:
16 oz. cream cheese
1/2 C sugar

Mix crust ingredients, reserve 2 cups and press the rest into a 9 x 13 pan. Bake 8-10 minutes at 350 degrees. Soften cheese and mix with rest of filling ingredients. Pour over baked crust, top with reserved crumbs. Bake 25-30 minutes at 350 degrees.

Serve white or rose wines with mild cheeses

Ginger Peachy Cheesecake
A little extra fussing and every bite worth it!

Crust:
3/4 C fine gingersnap crumbs
1 T sugar
3 T melted butter

Mix and press in 9 inch pie plate,
reserving 2 T for topping.

Filling:
2 eggs
1/2 C sugar
1/2 C milk
1/8 t salt
1 envelope unflavored gelatin
1/4 C cold water
1 8 oz. pkg. cream cheese
2 fresh peaches, or 4 canned
   halves
1/2 C whipping cream

Separate eggs, beat egg yolks in top of double boiler. Blend in sugar, milk and salt. Cook over boiling water until slightly thickened. Soften gelatin in cold water, blend into egg mixture and let it cool. Soften cheese in a large bowl, Blend in cooled egg mixture. Fold in sliced peaches. Beat egg whites until stiff, but not dry. Fold into mixture. Whip cream and fold into mixture. Pour into crust, garnish with crumbs and chill for several hours. Decorate with additional peach slices. 8 servings.

Family Cheese Favorites

99

Peanut Butter Pie
A quick and easy treat for peanut butter lovers

1 9 inch graham cracker crust
1 8 oz. pkg. cream cheese
1 C powdered sugar
3/4 C peanut butter (can use the
  nutty variety)
8 oz whipped topping

Soften cheese and blend with sugar. Add peanut butter and blend well. Fold in whipped topping. Spoon into crust and top with chopped peanuts. Chill. Serves 8.

Family Cheese Favorites

100
Cherry Cheese Pie

1 9 inch crumb crust
1 8 oz. pkg. cream cheese
1 can sweetened condensed milk
1/3 C lemon juice
1 t vanilla
1 can cherry pie filling or glaze

Beat softened cheese and milk, lemon juice and vanilla. Mix well. and pour into crust. Chill 2-3 hours. Spread on cherry topping and serve. Serves 8.

Glaze:
1/3 C sugar
1 T cornstarch
1 C pitted sour cherries
1/2 C cherry juice

Mix sugar and cornstarch. Add to juice and cook until thick and clear. Add cherries. Add a drop or two of red coloring if desired.

101

Apple Pizza
For brunch or dessert for a crowd.
Good to the last crumb!

Crust:
2¾-3 cups flour
1 pkg. dry yeast
3 T sugar
1 t salt
1/2 C water
1/4 C milk
1/4 C butter
1 egg

Apple Topping:
2 T butter
2 large cooking apples
1/2 C sugar
2 T flour
1 t cinnamon
Peel and slice apples thinly. Melt butter in skillet, add apples, sugar, flour and cinnamon. Simmer 15 minutes and cool.

Cheese topping:
4 oz. cream cheese
2 T sugar
1 T lemon juice
1/4 t nutmeg
Blend ingredients and set aside.

Streusel topping:
1/3 C flour
1/3 C sugar
1/4 cup soft butter
Mix and set aside.

Blend 1½ C flour, yeast, sugar and salt in a large mixer bowl. Heat water, milk, and butter until very warm. Add to flour mixture and beat 3 minutes. By hand, stir in enough flour to make a soft dough. Cover and let rise 15 minutes. Pat dough on a large oiled pizza pan forming a rim around edge. Spread on cheese filling, then apple filling over cheese, sprinkle with streusel topping. Cover and let rise for 15 minutes. Bake at 375 degrees, 25-30 minutes. Serve warm or cold. Serves 16.

102
Lo-Cal Cheese Cake

1/2 C fine graham cracker
 crumbs
4 t melted butter
1 C lo fat cottage cheese
2 8 oz. pkgs. Neufchatel cheese
3/4 C sugar
2 T flour
1¼ t vanilla
3 eggs
1/4 C skim milk
1 C fresh or frozen strawberries
1/2 C lo fat plain yogurt
2 t skim milk

Combine crumbs and butter and press in 8″ springform pan. Combine cheeses and beat with mixer. Add sugar, flour and vanilla, and mix until blended. Add eggs, one at a time and blend, but do not overbeat. Remove from mixer and stir in 1/4 C milk. Pour mixture over crumbs and bake at 375 degrees, 45 minutes. Cool, remove from pan. Top cake with strawberries and drizzle with topping of yogurt mixed with 2 T milk.

103
German Chocolate Cheese Cake

1 pkg. German Chocolate
cake mix

1/2 C coconut
1/2 C soft butter
4 eggs
3 8-oz. pkgs. cream cheese
1¼ C sugar
2 T vanilla
2 C sour cream

Combine cake mix, coconut, butter and one egg. Blend with mixer. Press this crust mixture into the bottom of a 13 x 9 inch pan. (reserve 1/3 cup for garnish, if desired). Combine cheese, three eggs, one cup sugar, one T vanilla. Beat until smooth and spread over crust. Bake at 350 degrees, 30 minutes or until set. While baking, combine sour cream with 1/4 C sugar, and one tablespoon vanilla. Remove cake from oven and spread with sour cream. Let cool at room temperature. Refrigerate overnight to enhance flavors. Sprinkle with reserved crumbs if desired.

104
Baked Cheese Cake
Rich and delicious

1/3 box graham crackers
1/3 C butter
1/3 C sugar
1 pt. sour cream
1/2 C sugar
1 t vanilla

Three 8 oz. pkg. cream cheese
5 eggs
1 C sugar
1 t vanilla

Crush graham crackers and mix with butter and sugar. Pat in bottom of 13 x 9 inch pan. Mix softened cheese, eggs, 1 C sugar, and vanilla. Pour over crust. Bake at 325 degrees, 40 minutes. While baking, mix sour cream, sugar and vanilla. Pour on hot cake. Return to oven for 5 minutes. Cool. Serves 16.

105

Pumpkin Cheese Cake

Dessert for your diet!

24 graham crackers
2 T margarine
4 t cocoa
1 T sugar
1/2 t cinnamon
3 eggs
1/2 C brown sugar
1½ C Ricotta cheese
1½ C canned pumpkin
1 C lo-fat cottage cheese
1 t pumpkin pie spice
1 t vanilla

Whipped topping

Combine crust ingredients. Press mixture on bottom and 1 inch up sides of 8 inch spring form pan. Bake at 425 degrees, 5 minutes. In mixer bowl, beat eggs, add sugar and blend well. Add rest of filling ingredients, beating well. Pour over crust. Bake at 425 degrees, 10 minutes. Reduce heat to 325 and bake one hour longer. Cool cake in pan. Serve with whipped topping. 12 servings, 55 calories per serving.

106
Nutty Cheese Tea Cake
Not too sweet, like pound cake

1 C butter
1½ C sugar
2 C flour
2 t baking powder
1/2 t salt
8 oz. cream cheese
1 t grated lemon rind
5 eggs
3/4 C chopped walnuts

1½ C finely chopped walnuts
2 T sugar
2 T butter

Blend ingredients and press on the bottom and sides of a 10 in. bundt pan. Bake at 400 degrees 6-8 minutes until nuts are brown. Cool.

Cream butter and cheese. Add sugar and lemon rind. Beat in eggs one at a time beating well after each addition. Add baking powder and salt to flour and gradually add to cheese mixture. Fold in nuts. Pour batter into prepared pan and bake at 300 degrees, 1¼ hours or until tests done. Cool for a few minutes, then invert on serving plate, and cool completely. Serves 12-16.

For best flavor, allow cheese to reach room temperature before serving

107
Cottage Custard Apple Pie

2 eggs
1/8 t salt
1/2 C sugar
1/2 C light cream
3/4 C milk
1 t vanilla
1 C cottage cheese
1½ C sliced apples
1/4 C sugar
1/4 t cinnamon
1/4 t nutmeg
1 10″ unbaked pieshell

Combine eggs, 1/2 C sugar, salt, cream, milk, vanilla, and cottage cheese. Set aside. Combine apples 1/4 C sugar and spices in pie shell. Bake at 425 degress, 15 minutes. Reduce heat to 325 and add custard mixture. Bake 40 minutes longer.

108
Chocolate Chip Cheesecake

Crust:
1-1/3 C vanilla wafer crumbs
3 T sugar
4 T melted butter

Combine and press into bottom of
9 inch springform pan.

Filling:
3 8-oz. pkgs. cream cheese
3/4 C sugar
1 t vanilla
3 eggs
1 C mini chocolate chips

Combine softened cream cheese
and sugar. Add eggs one at a time.
Blend in vanilla and chips. Bake
at 350 degrees, 35-45 minutes, or
until center is set. Cool in pan,
then chill. Serves 10.

109
Cream Cheese Brownies

Crust:
1 pkg. brownie mix
1/3 C milk
2 eggs

Filling:
1 8 oz. pkg. cream cheese
2 T butter
1/4 C sugar
1 T flour
1 egg
1/2 t vanilla

Icing:
1/2 C sugar
1/3 C milk
5 T butter
butter chips
12 oz. pkg. peanut butter chips

Blend brownie mix with milk and eggs. Spread 2/3 of batter in a greased 9 x 13 baking pan. Cream butter and cheese. Add rest of filling ingredients and mix well. Spread over batter in pan. Add the rest of the batter. Bake at 350 degrees, 35-40 minutes.

Heat sugar, milk and butter. Bring to a boil and boil 1 minute. Add chips. Cool and frost brownies.

110

Diabetic Cheese Tarts

1/2 C butter or margarine
1/2 C dry cottage cheese
1 C flour
1/2 t salt
Diabetic jam

Cream butter and cheese, add salt and flour. Form into a roll and chill for 30 minutes. Cut roll into 12 equal portions, flatten on floured board into 3 inch squares. Place a teaspoon of jam in center of square. Bring corners together and seal. Bake at 400 degrees, 10 minutes, or until lightly browned. 12 tarts. Exchanges: 1 tart equals 1/2 bread and 2 fat exchanges. 110 calories per tart.

Greek Feta cheese is made from ewe or goat's milk

Family Cheese Favorites